TOWARD A PEACEMAKERS ACADEMY

A PROPOSAL FOR A FIRST STEP TOWARD A UNITED NATIONS TRANSNATIONAL PEACEMAKING FORCE

by

ARTHUR I. WASKOW

1967

SPRINGER-SCIENCE+BUSINESS MEDIA, B.V.

ISBN 978-94-017-5634-1 ISBN 978-94-017-5886-4 (eBook)
DOI 10.1007/978-94-017-5886-4

Copies may be ordered through the World Association of World Federalists
Burg. Patijnlaan 49, The Hague, The Netherlands

Revised edition

Contents

	Page
A Note on Origins	5
Introduction and Summary	7
The Political Need	11
The Recent Experience	12
Private Action toward a New Vocation	16
The Curriculum	21
Morale	21
Languages	23
Policeman-Conciliator	25
Teacher-Community Organizer	28
Technical Skills	31
The Institution	35
The Academy in Operation	35
The Planning Stage	37
The Site	38
The Alumni	39
Conclusion	41

A Note on Origins

This study was first initiated by a committee of the World Association of World Federalists which was set up to study the kind of education other than military that will be necessary for the development of a wholly new kind of international force appropriate for peacekeeping and peacemaking, and to develop a plan or alternate plans that might facilitate the creation of such a force.

In the fall of 1966, the Committee asked the Institute for Policy Studies (an independent research and educational center in Washington, D.C.) to examine whether it would be desirable and possible to create a center for the training of international peacemakers. The Institute agreed to do the study, with the understanding that as in all its work, the Institute researchers would come to their own conclusions and would make the results available to the public generally. Arthur I. WASKOW, a Resident Fellow of the Institute and author of *The Limits of Defense*, *Keeping the World Disarmed*, and *From Race Riot to Sit-in*, directed the study, with the research assistance of Marilyn MCNABB. He is grateful to members of the Committee for their assistance and suggestions, and to a considerable number of experts on international education and international peacekeeping for their criticisms of drafts of this report. The responsibility for the views and estimates embodied in this final report is entirely his own.

Introduction and Summary

One of the most effective ways of pursuing social change is for men to imagine some future they would like to live within, and then act in the present to *create* some part of that future, not merely to plead for its creation. This proposal is based upon that process. It suggests the creation in the present of a specific institution designed to be one element in a certain kind of international future.

First, the proposal: We urge that, in order to prepare for a future institution under the United Nations auspices, private persons and organizations from a number of countries proceed to create a Peacemakers Academy, intended to train men and women for two years to enter a new profession of peacekeeping that would both deal with crises of outright violence that threatened world peace, and between such crises, deal with some of the chronic underlying problems that lead to violence. (It might also deal with natural disasters.) We suggest that the Peacemakers Academy assume for its early years a budget of about $1,000,000 a year and a student body of at least 500, both to be expanded as more money, teachers, and students become available. We propose that students of the Academy be taught to be multilingual and to some extent "multicultural"; that their loyalties to their home societies be softened and their loyalties to each other and to some sense of "the world" strengthened; that they be trained in basic police skills, including the careful use of limited weaponry in necessary circumstances; in civil engineering, both in rough makeshift style and in some cases at more "professional" levels; in public health and basic medicine; in teaching and community organizing; and in grass-roots mediation. Some of the persons to be admitted as students should already possess some relevant skill; others, especially from the Third World, may be coming straight from secondary school.

As to our image of the future: This proposal is based upon an analysis of international conflict which holds that within the next generation it is critically important for there to be a transnational peacekeeping and peace-creating agency –

transnational in the sense that it does not depend upon the support of national governments but upon groups and organizations of people that cut across national lines;

peacekeeping in the sense that it can cope with outright violence, domestic or international, which seems likely to lead toward international war;

peacecreating in the sense that it might help to meet some of the desperate needs for food, economic development, and a share in political power which now – unmet among many of the world's people – often lead to war.

As to the present act: To bring such a force into being, its members would have to be trained; and a special transnational Academy would have to be set up to train them. For the men who would work in such a service would be men of a new profession, with a new career line; and like all professionals, they would have to learn their craft. Such men scarcely exist today, though one can see the ancestry of their vocation scattered in a dozen different places: the American Seabee, the British Bobby, the Cuban militia-woman, the peace corpsman, the Shanti Sena nonviolent policeman, and the Red Cross worker. To make a whole training in this new profession out of odd bits and pieces, a new kind of Academy would be required. And it is this Academy that we think can now be built.

We suggest that it be done by private organizations, in order to get it done at once. Ultimately – the sooner the better, on condition that the United Nations achieves a universal membership – the UN should be responsible for such a school and for the Peacemakers it trains. But we believe such a relationship with the UN is more likely to be realized if the Academy is put together by private groups, and financed by foundations, private individuals, and perhaps a few governmental contributions, than if it must wait upon a formal UN initiative. We believe a useful first step toward opening the Academy would be the choice of two men who might become its administrators – perhaps, for example, an expert in peacemaking from Scandinavia and an expert in grass-roots economic development from a revolutionary African state. Such men could then push the plans forward. Perhaps a useful second step would be the bringing together for a summer planning and training session of about 15 of the kinds of men who might be its faculty and 15 of the kinds who might be students, many of whom might then become the cadre for the actual Board and Faculty of the Academy and would undertake to get it started.

In deciding on a site, the Academy's planners should take into account the factors of symbolic importance, neutral ground, educational usefulness, and financial attractiveness. On various of these grounds, special consideration might be given to such sites as Hiroshima, Algeria, Tanzania, the Expo '67 site in Canada, and Scandinavia.

One caveat: If the Academy is to serve the function for which it is designed, its planners must include representatives of the widest possible spectrum of political opinion in the world. Spokesmen for Chinese and Soviet interests, as well as spokesmen for American and Western European interests, should be included. Revolutionaries in the "Third" World – those called to mind by Tanzania, Cuba, North Vietnam – must be included along with those more congenial to most "Western" ears, like leading groups in Mexico or India. It might indeed be useful for individuals and groups from the small "neutrals" both of Europe and Afroasia (Sweden, Finland, Yugoslavia; Algeria, Cambodia) to have a "disproportionate" share in shaping the future of such an Academy. Under no conditions should the Academy be allowed to turn into a private or international experiment in counter-insurgency.

Indeed, the Academy should be based on the understanding that the violence that Peacemakers will try to end or prevent is not only the sudden open violence of war, but the covert and institutionalized violence of the status quo in societies that try starve or police into quiescence the groups and people that seek social change. That is why they cannot be merely Peacekeepers – for in much of the world gentlemen may cry peace, peace, but there is no true peace to keep. It must be sought.

We do not attempt to propose what guidelines the UN or the Academy's own Board should develop for the use of the graduate Peacemakers who emerge from the Academy we describe, nor do we expect that the UN can do without the present national contingents earmarked for UN use. We are suggesting a first transnational project in peacekeeping capable of training men to carry out some very important missions, but not intended to cope with every contingency.

We believe that the graduates of such an Academy would be one of the most useful groups of men in the world; and we urge that the steps necessary to create them be taken now.

The Political Need

Both from a theory of the future and from an evaluation of the recent past, we believe that the world already needs, and within the next generation will be able to have, a transnational peacekeeping force. We think that such a force should both be able to bring outright violence to an end when it threatens to lead toward international war, and be able to begin to meet the desperate needs that in much of the world lead straight to war. We shall take up our evaluation of the past below; but first we shall quickly sketch our theory of the future.

We believe that during the next generation, it may be possible to create a world in which the nations carry on their conflicts without war – even though the conflicts survive, and indeed are occasionally carried on by all means short of war. We believe such a world would require nations to invent unarmed ways of carrying on their foreign policies, and to create an international organization capable of preventing a rearmament race.* But we also believe that to live in peace and to begin building the institutional framework that might make a world order possible, such a world would need to have institutions and organizations that could cut across the intense conflicts between nations – institutions that might be said to embody the growing edge of Mankind. Such organizations, set up not by the national governments but by private groups working together across national boundaries, might be called "transnational" agencies. ("International" agencies are those created by the national governments.)

Such transnational groups would be able to "surround", inhibit, and check the actions of national governments that might move toward rearmament or that, through imposing extreme injustice, might provoke violence. They would need real power to do so – not governmental power, but the power that arises out of public commitment: the power of fact-finding, of consumer economic pressure, of moral suasion. If they did not

* See ARTHUR I. WASKOW, *Keeping the World Disarmed* (Center for the Study of Democratic Institutions, 1965), for a discussion of how such a world might work.

have such power, it might be extremely hard to prevent conflicts from turning into skirmishes, skirmishes into rearmament races, and rearmament races into war.

If such transnational institutions need to be built, now is the time to build them. And we believe that one such institution is a Peacemaking Force that can not only deal with the eruptions of outright violence that endanger world peace, but work at the heart of the desperation that provokes such violence.

It is not only this particular image of the future that should urge upon us the creation of a transnational force of Peacemakers. Many who hold a different vision of the future might well agree that such a force is needed in the present. For the need emerges from any clear look at the recent past.

The Recent Experience

On practically every occasion in which a UN peacekeeping force has been found both necessary and feasible, the crisis has boiled up out of the desperate politics – nationalist, poverty-stricken and poverty-obsessed – of the underdeveloped world. In many cases, perhaps, the Great Powers by their military, economic or political behavior have stimulated the trouble. But when the trouble finally came, its public explosion was in the "Southern" world – whether it was the border between Israel and Egypt or the towns of the Congo or the huts of West Irian. The UN police have been hastily assembled after the explosion to damp it down, patrol borders or perform civilian police work. As the immediate threat of border war subsides, attention in the UN turns elsewhere. But for the inhabitants of the trouble spot, the poverty persists, their desperation deepens, the danger of violence continues, and the waste of life and talent accumulates as immeasurable and irrecoverable loss. Even if the UN force has succeeded in keeping the peace – temporarily – no one is making peace more durable. And no international service is acting to prevent a similar outbreak elsewhere.

Take Cyprus. The trouble between Greek and Turkish communities has persisted for centuries, exacerbated recently by the problems of transition from colonial status to that of a poverty-ridden independent nation caught by geography in threatening tensions of international power politics. After study of attitudes of both Greek and Turkish communities on the island, Malvern LUMSDEN of the International Peace Research Institute of Oslo concluded:

> The situation in Cyprus now (May, 1965) is that there are two communities, both with a tradition of "heroism," both with experience of violence in the pursuit of political ends, and both with outside political and material support. Both communities are largely committed to incompatible political objectives; both since December 1963 have used and threatened force in the pursuance of these objectives.

LUMSDEN proposed that this trouble spot not be permitted to "disappear" from international consciousness when the fighting stopped (as most of it did stop after a 6,000-man UN force was interposed between the belligerents), but that immediate and long-term economic, educational, and cultural and social programs be directed toward the end of *peacemaking*. Looking to the next generation of Greeks and Turks sharing the island, he suggests a thirty-year perspective for the job.

In the urgent moment of outright violence, ending the danger to civilian populations and the danger of spreading warfare may require a number of military or para-military actions summarized as follows by the Washington Center of Foreign Policy Research paper, "The Future Character and Role of Peace Observations Arrangements" (pp. 11, 12):

The quasi-military tasks include:

a. establishment of cease-fires, truces and sometimes armistices to obtain cessation of fighting.

b. establishment of demarcation lines.

c. establishment of demilitarized zones on one or both sides.

d. observation of the demarcation lines to determine the responsibility for violations and to suggest the treatment of violations.

e. reporting on the disengagement of opposing forces and occasionally interposing between the forces to insure their disengagement.

f. observing and assisting in the withdrawal or demobilization of forces.

g. observing bans on the introduction of fresh troops or arms in an area or the establishment of military bases.

h. arranging for the exchange of prisoners of war and civilian internees.

Typical quasi-political tasks of peace-observation missions have included:

a. reporting on the political conditions existing in the area.

b. radio monitoring to determine the existence and extent of external interference in an area.

c. arranging for the exchange of civilian populations after the establishment of a boundary of demarcation line.

d. in a few instances arranging for the transfer of territory from one state to another.

e. assistance in assuring the enforcement of treaty provisions guaranteeing democratic freedoms in an area.

f. supervision of national elections.

g. reporting on the observation of provisions in international treaties calling for the "neutrality" of an area.

In addition, there are other but equally urgent needs to be met once the outright violence has been brought under control: resettlement of refugees, rebuilding of homes, schools, and other damaged property, provision of sanitation and medical relief – requiring skills and supplies immediately. LUMSDEN stresses that it is important to involve the local population in these tasks and, further, that the "short-term restoration programme must therefore be linked to the long-term development programme not only for the efficiency of the whole process, but also so that the people can feel themselves actively participating in the construction of their own worthwhile future."

United Nations experience in peacekeeping operations has developed in the last twenty years from a series of *ad hoc* and in large part experimental arrangements. UN personnel have moved into – and out of – emergencies in Greece, Palestine, Kashmir, Suez and Gaza, Lebanon, Jordan, the Congo, West Irian, Yemen, and Cyprus with a wide variety of mandates, objectives, and levels of success. From these and other operations, some patterns and standards have emerged. For example, it was apparent to the UN Commission evaluating the work of the Congo force that the Nigerian soldier's skills in keeping down outbreaks of violence with a minimum of force made them particularly adept at peacekeeping. Still, the uncertainties of *ad hoc* combinations of contingents of soldiers speaking different languages, holding different loyalties and trained in different organizations of command has created distracting and sometimes embarrassing problems. Contingents have been withdrawn when their national governments change policy; contingents from different nations have pursued conflicting policies that reduced the effectiveness of the total UN force; there have been difficulties in establishing firm command lines over hastily assembled diverse units talking different languages, both literally and figuratively; where a given force has been heavily dominated by contingents from one or few nations, it has been laid open to charges of bias by the parties in conflict or other UN members.

From these experiences, it became apparent that even within the assumption that a UN force should only focus on putting out critical brushfires of outright violence, some major changes should be made. First of all, policemen were more relevant than soldiers; secondly, a standing force that was instantly available would be a considerable help. But neither of these changes could be easily achieved.

On the first point, it seemed clear that the skills of policemen trained to isolate violent individuals or small groups and restore order, or to patrol a border against infiltration, were more likely to be needed than the skills of soldiers trained to conquer and hold a territory and overawe its whole population, or to repel an invading army. Yet the UN found there were considerable political difficulties involved in trying to ask for policemen, instead of soldiers, from member nations. Few countries have a surplus of policemen, and few have institutional arrangements for transferring policemen from their regular duties and shipping them five thousand miles on a moment's notice. So some member nations began to earmark military units for possible UN use, and to train these units more nearly as policemen; and some made a few policemen available, to work with military units in peacekeeping operations. These developments offer great hope for the future, but they do not preclude taking other steps to provide a multipurpose peacekeeping force.

On the second point, the need for instantaneous responses to crises, for development of an effective line of command to which units would be ready to respond, and for establishing loyalties or obediences to the UN rather than particular national governments (to prevent sudden withdrawals of units or contradictory orders) seemed all to urge creation of a standing UN force. But there were serious political objections and difficulties. The low level of political consensus in the world – and particularly the suspicions and hostilities between the great powers, in part growing out of anger among some of them over how previous UN forces were used – makes it very difficult for the UN to make the political decision to create a standing force that one or more of the great powers fears it cannot control, though in the emergency of a given crisis the great-power members of the UN have frequently been willing to create and use a force. Moreover, some members have felt that a standing force would be too expensive, since it would do nothing between war crises but would cost just as much money then as when it moves into action. And some military experts have warned that the force itself, if a "standing" rather than an emergency group, would be plagued by feelings of boredom and uselessness.

Moreover, if we look beyond the control of outright violence to the building of conditions of stable peace from such emergencies it is even more apparent that the UN needs some new tools. Only a non-UN group, for example, attempted to do any grass-roots conciliation in Cyprus. LUMSDEN points out that an international voluntary workcamp which in August, 1965, worked on improving a road to the benefit of both Turkish and Greek farmers might tentatively be considered "a tiny extension to the work of the UN force." In creating a project on which members of both sides of the conflict worked together for mutual advantage and through personal and group initiatives of friendship to local residents, work camp members conducted a small experiment in peacekeeping. LUMSDEN's study of attitudes toward the UN force in Cyprus indicated that UN servicemen had no contact – except visual – with the people they were protecting. To Greek and Turkish Cypriots, the guarding force looks "weak" and "passive." Perhaps in more positive roles, more like those created by members of the work camp, the UN force's popular image would improve. Since UN authority usually depends much more on respect than sheer military power, skill in group conflict resolution could be a significant asset to the force's effectiveness and to local confidence in that effectiveness.

We are not suggesting that "grass-roots goodwill" can substitute for the reaching of basic political agreements between parties in conflict, nor that grass-roots goodwill can survive the explosion of basic political differences into violence ordered or encouraged by hostile governments. But we are arguing that in areas of chronic distress rather than explosive crisis, the slow and patient building of connections between hostile communities and of solutions for age-old problems of poverty and despair can make it more likely that political agreements can be reached and the decision for war never be reached. The skills needed for long-term peace-creating in such chronic situations and short-term peace-restoring in a crisis may be somewhat different but we believe that they overlap and the same people can be trained to fill both roles, as the situation demands.

UN specialized agencies have counted, analyzed, published and planned for the complex problems of developing nations, but the working link between peacekeeping and developmental work has been realized only in isolated projects. For example, the UN mission in the Congo included civilian operations – from UN engineers repairing a breakdown in the water system, to the WHO doctors and smallpox vaccination teams visiting isolated villages to longer-range training programs. But the richest source of experience in creating the working link between peacemaking and community development is probably that of private organizations. For example, organizations like the International Red Cross, the United Nations Associations, and the various Friends Service Committees have considerable experience with international voluntary work camps and longer-term developmental projects in tension areas. Their knowledge as well as that of national youth exchange and service programs like the various national "peace corps," Operation Crossroads Africa, Commission on Ecumenical Voluntary Service Projects and other church-related programs, International Voluntary Service, the American Field Service, the Experiment in International Living and similar organizations will be valuable in designing future international programs – in language training, for example, and recruitment procedures – for the kind of work LUMSDEN proposes, though he stresses the advantages of UN auspices.

Private Action toward a New Vocation

Suppose that one accepts that a transnational force able to deal with the underlying problems of desperate poverty, racial or cultural suspicions, and historic exclusion from participation in the political process would be desirable on its own account, because it would reduce the chances of a violent outbreak instead of merely suppressing the violence once it had erupted. Even so, could such a force meet the difficulties outlined above that have stood in the way of achieving a standing force, especially one with police rather than military skills? We suggest that it might more nearly deal with these problems. For one thing, such a force would be nearer to the civilian populace and much more easily trainable in the careful peacekeeping typical of the police than would be men in military units; indeed the police function is much more closely related to such work than is the army. Secondly, a standing force that did development work, grassroots conciliation of dangerous conflicts, and disaster relief as well as policing when necessary would have a continuous mission. Its cost, instead of being a drain on world budgets, would constitute an investment that many governments could than "afford." It would build a world-wide fund of political good will if it could assist areas struck by disasters like the Agadir earthquake or the Cuban hurricanes. Thirdly, because such a force would both be "doing" things and learning skills continuously between war emergencies, its own men would be involved, not bored; and governments whose citizens enlisted would see the Force as a training ground both for those men and for the people in various countries whom the force would train as part of its regular work.

But perhaps the greatest obstacle in the path of creating a standing peacekeeping force – even one capable of acting in between crises as well as during them – is the political difficulty of getting the great powers to agree to creating a force that might be used in ways they would not approve of. We suggest that this difficulty be met by starting the peacekeepers through private, non-governmental initiative. Such a force (which might be started by opening a school to train volunteers in the necessary skills, the graduates of which would make up the force) would bypass the political problem of getting the UN to found the force. Groups of the trained men could then be made available (a) to countries that wanted them (perhaps with the approval of the UN or of the Academy's own board to rule out misuse of the force by a government against its people), on a regular basis for development work, disaster relief, or reducing the level of internal conflict that threatened to erupt into violence, or already had; and (b) to the UN in emergencies when it was anxious to have peacekeepers available. The men would already be trained, be working together, have acceptable lines of authority, etc.

Is it possible for the new profession we propose to be created simply by training men in it, or is there some intrinsic difficulty in teaching men to be, simultaneously, policemen, conciliators, peace corpsmen, and disaster relief workers? We believe there is no such problem. As evidence, we would cite Hugh HANNING's report, "The Peaceful Uses of Military Forces" for the World Veterans Federation (Paris, 1966), which describes the "civilian" skills presently incorporated in national military training programs in Belgium, Brazil, Colombia, France, India, Iran, Israel, Ivory Coast, Morocco, the Netherlands, Nigeria, Pakistan, Peru, Thailand, the U.K. and the U.S. HANNING, a veteran of the British navy in World War II and an experienced journalist, summarized the range of technical skills now employed by army personnel in projects he observed in these sixteen countries as follows:

> Troop labour is suitable for the construction of simple irrigation systems; for the reclamation of land and draining of swamps; for the planting and harvesting of crops; for constructing, repairing, or improving roads, railroads and airfields; and for evacuating people from disaster areas. In the field of health, non-technical troops can help to improve sanitary standards, to devise acceptable methods of disposing of human waste; to eradicate malaria and other insect-transmitted diseases; and to provide safe water supplies. In education, those who are literate can help to provide basic training. In community development, they can prepare plans and engage in the construction of schools, civil centres; and they can help initially to operate some of these projects.

Often, they will be working under or alongside engineer units; but their assistance can be of great value...

With more expert and technical training available, the range of work is similarly wide:

...grading operations; setting up and operating machinery such as sawmills; devising and constructing flood controls; designating, designing and supervising the construction of buildings; providing larger-scale water supplies... the installation, operation and maintenance of telephone, telegraph and radio systems; and the setting up and operation of emergency communications centres, especially in time of disaster... help in the movement of agricultural produce, seeds and fertilizers; disaster relief; and road building... increasing or improving the production of animals, grain or vegetables... (Chapter III, p. 8).

Health, nutrition, child care and other educational activities could easily be added to the list were the recruits to include women and training expanded to include wives of volunteers. HANNING discusses the importance of projects that stimulate self-help, the need for "outsiders" to work *with* rather than for local communities. National programs in Iran and Israel have been especially effective in catalyzing local participation in development programs. For Americans, perhaps the Seabees – the Navy's Construction Battalion – is the most familiar case of men trained to fight when necessary, but usually to build bridges, teach public-health measures, improvise machinery, etc. If such skills as soldiery, teaching, and doctoring can be combined, there seems no reason to doubt that the "new profession" we are proposing can be taught and used, if the effort is made.

What is lacking, then, to create the sort of peace-making force prescribed specifically for Cyprus but relevant to many developing areas is an institution able to transmit and develop the experience now existing within and outside the UN to men and women who can be available to move immediately into a needy country, a natural disaster area, or a crisis situation and begin the work of helping victims and belligerents to help themselves. That such an Academy should be transnational and UN-oriented seems logical. In the absence of a UN decision, such a school could be initiated by private sources and its graduates made available to the UN as a new kind of peacekeeping force. If it proved its worth, ultimately such a privately initiated school would probably itself be adopted or copied by the UN. The important thing is to bring into existence an institution – around which would then grow both rules for its own governance, and rules for the use of its graduates as a peacekeeping force.

No private group could be successful in creating an Academy unless it were itself "transnational": that is, cut across national and ideological boundaries to bring together men who despite other differences, agreed on the need for the Peacemakers. Some churches, labor movements, political movements, and business associations are prime examples of such transnational groups; but just as relevant to the problems of a Peacekeepers

Academy are the private associations that focus on the need for cross-national and supranational political institutions.

Once such a group of persons from such organizations had taken on the task of beginning a school for peacekeepers, the staff of the UN Secretariat and of specialized UN agencies could provide advice, resources, guidelines, training, and perhaps personnel. But even then there would probably be advantages to keeping the Peacemakers Academy a distinct institution, separate from the UN's other work and agencies (such as UNITAR, intended to train international civil servants and do peace research), though drawing upon such agencies where necessary. A mere collection of international scholarships or university exchanges might conceivably produce the minimal necessities of language, vocational, and technical training, yet not produce a cohesive international peacekeeping force. If a force is ever to act together in the field effectively, it will need precisely the *esprit de corps* that previous UN forces have been able to build only late and painfully if at all, on the spot of conflict and after they were assembled. A campus would also permit the possibility of leisure-time exploration by students and faculty in experimenting with direct cross-cultural interpretation and exchange, with possibly rich but little-explored potentials for peace-making.

The Curriculum

The crucial fact about the curriculum of a Peacemakers Academy is that the Academy will have to learn from its own mistakes and successes, and alumni will have to be constantly feeding back to the Academy what they have learned from their work, in order to enrich and change its teaching. The Academy's students should from the beginning be as deeply engaged as possible in the kind of work they will do after graduation: the Academy ought to be almost as much a project in peacekeeping as a training center for it. But although we must insist on an open-ended curriculum, it is necessary to start somewhere; and it seems possible to identify some of the skills that an effective peacekeeper would need to have. Moreover, it seems useful to spell out as much as possible what the Academy might look like, in order to dispel the vagueness that naturally attends a proposal to create a new kind of school for a new kind of profession. We will have to keep in mind that we expect such detailed descriptions to be incorrect or become incorrect soon after the Academy opens: its procedures will change according to experience.

Morale

Perhaps the most important "skill" for Peacemakers would be a certain kind of *esprit de corps* – built around an emotional ruggedness and creative intelligence under pressure that would be absolutely necessary in crisis situations and highly desirable even in the lonely work of a village community-organizing team. "Teaching" these traits is a matter of the whole *gestalt* of the Academy, but certain specifics can be identified.

One way of starting men off with high unit morale is to have a rigorous selection system, so that all who start at the Academy feel that they and their comrades are already the pick of the world for this particular job. Such a standard seems not to be absolutely essential – one of the great high-morale units in history was the French Foreign Legion, which imposed no such selection process – but when there is added to this factor the one that in a small Academy, it would be only economical to keep flunk-outs and drop-outs to a minimum, rigorous selection seems indicated. Of course, the Foreign Legion's public myths of ultra-boldness at the edge of the world and of the fed-up Legionnaire who chose to enlist instead of committing suicide (or after committing murder), probably acted as a kind of selection test – keeping out the inappropriate possibilities. An analogous myth would presumably begin to grow out of the real work of Peacemakers, and such a myth should deliberately be fostered. All students should, of course, be volunteers – rather, for example, than men from a national army who had been assigned to the Academy.

The kinds of standards that should be set high – the capabilities to be considered crucial for a Peacemaker – should include such emotional traits as personal independence and initiative, the ability to "step back" from a quarrel in progress rather than identifying with one side, and the ability to act with "presence" and firmness in a crisis; some intellectual capacities (probably not "academic" in style) such as facility with languages and perhaps multicultural experience; perhaps some few political or attitudinal characteristics such as relatively low commitment to any national government; and the physical ruggedness necessary to cope with sudden departures from a peaceful village to an explosive border town 5,000 miles away, there to work long hours as a policeman under trying conditions.

Once students have begun their work/study as apprentice Peacemakers, the Academy should find the traditional builders of *esprit de corps* most useful: rituals and ceremonies, sports and games, music. Considering the kind of men the Academy would want to turn out, it might well be that its rituals would have to be open-ended and continuously self-created, rather than centrally, formally, and permanently established. (A loose analogy would be the way in which within Quaker ritual, each member of a Meeting House speaks his own mind rather than reciting some traditional, agreed-on text. Yet the sense of occasion and ritual is accomplished. For an Academy bringing together men of extremely different political, religious, and cultural backgrounds, some such ritual of diversity-within-unity might have to be developed. Perhaps there would then emerge some items of ceremony that all students could accept into a tradition – a song, a memorial to Peacemakers killed during a mission, etc.)

One way of emphasizing personal commitment of students to the Academy and its band of alumni (as well as decreasing political strains between the Peacemakers and populations they work among) might be to enlist both men and women – perhaps to enlist a considerable proportion of married couples. The prejudice against using women in military or quasi-military roles seems to have been conquered in forces like the Israeli army and the Cuban militia; and their more traditional skills in nursing and grassroots conciliation would seem most pertinent to the kind of Peacemaking force we are proposing. But perhaps the most telling argument for such an arrangement is that if men are expected to enlist for 10 or 20 years of service around the world, on constant emergency call and continuous semi-emergency duty that keeps them much more on the move than any traditional soldier but also much more likely to be planted in an alien land for a year or two, it seems likely that the only two workable arrangements would be the enlistment of married couples, or an oath of chastity like that of the mendicant friars of Europe and Asia. The strains traditionally incident to the quartering of a group of bachelor males on a civilian population would be less acceptable for a Peacemakers force than they have been either for an army mobilized in its own homeland or for an army that has occupied a conquered country. The obvious problem with enlisting married couples is dealing with the possibility of children; but that problem should be weighed against the benefits suggested above.

It might be useful, both for purposes of morale and for the better melding of different skills, to arrange that Peacemakers would on graduation from the Academy (if not before) be grouped into teams of somewhere between six and ten members who would stay together, at least for several years. Such a team could work for two years on community development in (for example) the Southern Sudan, incidentally trying to knit together into co-operative action some of the conflicting ethnic groups there, could spend six weeks at the Academy to teach and learn anew, could return to the Sudan and then on an hour's notice fly elsewhere to deal with a sudden increase of border incidents there. Its members would know how to work together and would need less time to deal with a sudden new set of orders, and their social reinforcement of each other would strengthen their loyalty to the Peacemakers rather than particular countries – their own or those they worked among. The groups could be reshuffled after three or four years together, perhaps mixing veterans into younger groups just leaving the Academy.

Languages

Of the more formal curriculum of the Academy, perhaps most urgent would be training in languages. Depending on the pool of available talent, applicants might be required to be fluent in speaking at least two languages, at least one of which was in wide use across the world; and students might be required to learn to speak one or two or more languages during their two years at the Academy. It would seem reasonable, considering the world political configuration in which English is the nearest there is to the lingua franca that Peacemakers might need, to require that all students know English from the start, in addition to their mother tongue; and that English-speakers know some other world language from the start. Students might also be required to choose among Arabic, Spanish, French, Swahili, Portuguese, Hindi-Urdu, and perhaps Malay – the languages most likely to be needed, besides English, in peacekeeping as well as community-development operations. (Russia and China seem not likely to be sites of international peacekeeping or international development efforts in the next several decades.) Thus every Peacemaker would on leaving the Academy speak fluently three or four languages, one of which was English and at least one other spoken by a considerable part of the world's population.

The teaching of the third or third-and-fourth languages should be aimed very heavily at speaking and hearing it, with moderate attention to reading, and little to writing, and none to the theory or "grammar" of the language. In the areas which the Peacemakers would be operating, literacy would in any case probably be low and conversation far more important than print.

The use of films and tapes of instructors in other subjects who normally use and would also teach the required languages could get the necessary education done rather easily in the allotted two years. Peace Corps experience indicates that the American trainee with "average" language aptitude requires 400 hours of training to have control of Spanish or Portuguese satisfactory enough that most remaining difficulties disappear within a month after his arrival overseas.(With 300 hours of training, it took six months in the field to reach the same level.) The Defense Language Institute at Monterey, California, runs courses in French of 12 and 24 weeks, in Malay and Arabic of 47 weeks, and expects students to spend 30 hours a week in class and 15 in study at home. These times could probably be reduced, and performance improved, if high language aptitude were one of the crucial requirements for admission to the Academy.

The language teaching would require a wide variety of instructors – for example, an engineer who was fluent in French, Arabic, and English; a public health expert fluent in Swahili and Portugese; a former UN peace-force commander who had Hindi and English; etc. It would also require the use of tapes and movies, most of which could probably be supplied cheaply or free by some of the world's leading universities and defense establishments.

Along with the languages themselves, students should be learning about the cultures that go along with them. Much of this information could be combined with language learning, by discussing the relevant history and social system in the relevant language. More concentrated attention could be paid to a given culture in the last stages of the two-year course, when students know what their first assignment will be, just before they take off into a particular project. Some, of course, will be learned after arrival in the field. But one way or the other, effective peacekeepers must be sensitive to the processes of the conflict they are trying to lessen, and will therefore have to understand the nuances of the behavior that they meet.

If they have been able to internalize such information, and perhaps more important if they are "quick studies" in it, they should be able in emergencies to bring together the two roles that at first glance look so disparate: policeman and conciliator. Some analysts have suggested that training a man to hold a firm quasi-military bearing and training him in the art of compromise are incompatible. But there is some evidence that the two "contradictory" jobs have in recent years been growing toward each other. One can see this on the one hand in the attempt to teach "human relations" to American policemen confronting intense racial hostilities in large cities, and on the other hand in the training of Gandhian conciliators as a nonviolent-intervention police in India's Shanti Sena. And the situations which have given rise to both developments – the eruption of outright violence between ethnic groups both considered to be part of the body politic, and therefore neither liable to be simply crushed – are exactly the kinds of situations which either between or within nations, have triggered the desire for an international peacekeeping force. It is because the world community wants to end border raids between Arabs and Israelis or mutual slaughter between Greek and Turkish Cypriots or among different Congolese tribal groups and Belgian soldiers, *without treating either side as the enemy*, that the peacekeeper concept has come to replace that of the original UN Charter's military coercion.

Policeman-Conciliator

What sort of training is involved in the converging roles of policeman and conciliator? First of all, it is clear that the weaponry that should be made available to a policeman (as distinct from a soldier) and especially to the conciliatory policeman should be most carefully limited. Peacemakers are intended to prevent violence or halt it, not escalate it. Mass-destruction or indiscriminate weapons like modern high explosives, napalm, biological warfare, or nuclear shells are clearly outside the legitimate line. Every effort should be bent toward using the most precise and least lethal weapons available. Whatever the dangers of escalation in lethal chemical warfare that arise from the confrontation of national armies that claim to be using non-lethal gases, it seems likely that an international force of Peacemakers would want to have available truly nonlethal chemicals, and to exclude from its arsenal all lethal chemicals: an arrangement analogous to the police use of tear gas for dispersing rioters in many modern states. So far as the use of such agents in actual peacekeeping is concerned, the necessary distinctions should probably be made by some formal international body like the UN or the Permanent Court of International Justice; but the Academy could make provisional judgments so far as training is concerned. (A useful test might be that a "non-lethal" chemical is one that the students would not mind using on each other in training.) Lethal but relatively discriminate weapons such as small arms and rifles would also be needed in the arsenal of the Peacemakers. On almost all occasions, the Peacemakers should be under strictures to avoid the use of such weapons – and indeed in Gaza and Cyprus, and during most of the UN operation in the Congo, weapons were rarely used. But occasions when they seemed to be needed did occur, and unless the Academy were prepared to go all the way with a nonviolent discipline, the men should be trained in the use of limited weaponry.

Simultaneously, however, the training of Peacemakers must focus on how to avoid needing to resort to weaponry. In a basic course for municipal police officers given by New York State, of 210 classroom hours 25 are devoted to training in the use of firearms. For comparison, other important chunks are given to learning the laws of arrest (14 hours), criminal procedures (14 hours), the nature of crime (21 hours), emergency aid to persons (14 hours), the police and public disorder (12 hours); and human relations (8 hours). In New York's intermediate course, the weight is even more heavily against training in the use of weaponry. Of 80 hours, 20 are given to relations between police and the public, 20 to study of the penal code and the nature of the police and court system, and 20 to police techniques of which the use of weaponry is only part. The policeman as neighborhood conciliator, investigator, and observer is more and more the ideal – if not yet the reality. In some other societies, of course, this outlook has been even stronger. The London police, for example, may not deserve every item of their reputation, but it is clear that they resort to the carrying of firearms, and therefore their use, only on extremely rare occasions.

It should be made clear that our proposal to train Peacemakers who cannot resort to major force is not intended to exclude the creation or earmarking of more "military" units which could be brought to bear in case of extreme emergency like the UN's decision to "conquer" Katanga. The forces presently being trained for use by several Scandinavian countries, Canada, and the Netherlands would play precisely such roles. But if the experience since 1955 is any indication, they will be needed less often than the more conciliatory Peacemakers, and usually the need for them will become clear only if the Peacemakers try first, and fail at, the skills of conciliation.

What then are these skills? We must turn to the roles of labor-management conciliators in the United States, International Affairs Representatives of the various Quaker organizations in such circumstances as divided Berlin, and the Shanti Sena in India to understand. The skills all these sort of people use are those of patient and sensitive listening, restating the goals of opponents so that each side can understand the other's position and know precisely where the disagreements are and where possible agreements could begin, splitting over-arching conflicts up into specific disputes the "winning" or "losing" of which seems much less threatening or essential to the parties, representing and affirming through their own stance the "humanness" of both sides to the dispute in situations where the conflict spiral has gone so far that each side is denying that the other is human, and strengthening on each side the conflict-resolving forces most willing to look toward "help" from conflict resolvers on the other side.*

* See Roger FISHER, "Fractionating Conflict" and Morton DEUTSCH, "Producing Change in an Adversary" in Roger FISHER, ed., *International Conflict and Behavioral Science* (Basic Books, 1964); Roland L. WARREN, "The Conflict Intersystem and the Change Agent,"

Training in these skills is chiefly a matter of constant experience; reading and discussing historical or theoretical analyses of conflict resolution may point to certain useful practices, but cannot teach people how to use them. Somewhat more helpful may be reading about and discussing in detail case studies of examples of successful conflict reduction, but by far the most useful learning will be actual participation of Academy students in dealing with real ethnic or labor conflicts. For this reason, it may be important to place the Academy in an area of known conflict that is expected to continue – a decision that might pay the double dividend of training the students more effectively and over the long run easing some important world trouble situation.

To the degree that it is difficult for students to learn conciliation through fieldwork, the Academy should fully use the technique of "simulation gaming." In this method, teachers set up a situation analogous to a real-life conflict and ask students to play to the hilt the roles of the parties involved in the conflict. Thus at international governmental level, simulation gaming would have students play the roles of Cabinet officers of great powers, the leadership of the UN and of important semi-private interests like the international oil companies or the "gnomes of Zurich" or the world Communist movement, of public pressure groups within various nations, and of conciliators and Peacemakers. The teachers invent a crisis situation and describe it in full to the students, who then take up their assigned roles and play the situation through to some kind of resolution. With such an arrangement, students learn not only how the conflict itself feels to the parties in conflict and how interests they have never felt part of (such as world banking interests, for an Indian medical student; the Chinese revolutionary leadership, for a Norwegian lawyer's daughter) would respond to an international crisis, but also how conciliators might deal with the problem. At a different level, the same technique could be used to simulate the clashes of Turkish and Greek Cypriot farmers, or Arab and Israeli border-dwellers, or merchants and villagers in Kerala. In the process of the game, students would learn to sharpen their perceptions of masked concessions, identify peripheral interests and power groups that could be brought into the situation to restrain hotheads, strenghten their ability to preserve a bearing of firmness and calmness under extreme circumstances, learn what the pressures of lost sleep, rumor, and fear do to parties in a conflict, and begin to invent their own methods of coping with all these problems. The atmosphere of the simulations could range from the bureaucratic but bloody-minded deliberations of government officials in a crisis to the physical violence of street mobs in collision – since the Peacemakers are likely to confront the whole spectrum during their tour of duty. In the process, it should be pointed out, students would be absorbing information about the history,

Journal of Conflict Resolution VIII, no. 3, 231–241; Narayan DESAI, "A Note on Training in Nonviolence," Marjorie SYKES, "Training for Nonviolent Action."

politics, and social-psychological assumptions of the groups whose roles they play; and many simulations should probably be played through in the languages of the countries or areas in which the simulated conflicts occur.

Such simulations would not require elaborate computerization, as do some simulations now used by American academic and research centers, because their intention would not be to reflect in detail the comparative wealth, strength, etc, of real countries or to achieve a theoretical model of conflict processes, but to teach practical means of conflict reduction to the participants. They would therefore more nearly parallel the field "maneuvers" now carried on by armed forces of many nations.

For the performance of both the more police-oriented and the more conciliation-oriented tasks of peacekeeping, members of the force are likely to require training in the skills of physical reconnaissance and observation, ranging from binoculars to the observation helicopter. In addition, part of the corps may need to be taught techniques of non-physical inspection and intelligence such as budget checks, analysis of newspaper and similar data, and other means of analyzing what might be going on in a situation similar to that of Katanga, where private businesses, foreign governments, and underground political movements are operating in contravention of UN resolutions or regulations. Computer analysis, for example, might be a crucial element in training corpsmen who might be assigned such tasks. (There would probably not be many.)

Teacher-Community Organizer

Aside from the direct peacekeeping skills appropriate to situations that have already exploded into violence or are on the verge of doing so, we may examine the training that would be required of men who would usually be working in situations of buried violence – hunger, disease, despair. Here the more technical skills of medicine and engineering seem particularly appropriate, along with the semi-political, semi-technical skills of the teacher and community organizer.

The latter skills are most nearly cognate to those of the peacekeeper, since they focus on the relations between human beings rather than their bodies or their artefacts. And although it would seem the teacher (if not the community organizer) has a body of technical information to impart, a great deal of his skill is being able to turn students on, get them to want to learn the information they most need and want to know. In this sense it overlaps with community organizing, which is *par excellence* the job of turning people on. The organizer brings the knowledge that it is possible for a body of people to work together to achieve a useful end – a bit of information that has been drained out of or beaten out of many a peasant village or a desperate barrio in the underdeveloped world, at least insofar as achieving economic change and a share of national political power is concerned.

The skills needed for getting across this information have been effectively summarized by Frank MANKIEWICZ, former regional director for Latin America of the US Peace Corps:

The community organizers must be trained to observe, to notice, to write down what they see and to compile and to draw conclusions from the information they have. They've got to be able to spend their first three or four months finding out where they are and who their neighbors are and what is going on here. Who are all these people, where did they come from and what do they want? Who has the power? Who is the *alcalde*? How did he get to be the *alcalde*? Is he really chief of this community? Who is the school teacher and where does he come from and is this assignment as teacher in this village a demotion or a promotion? Where was he before? If he had a good city post and now he has a slum post, he's going to be resentful. Why did he get demoted? Is he in the wrong political party? Will he get promoted again? Can he do you any good? Who runs the bar? Why does everyone talk to this person and not to that person? These two people have the same name – are they related? There are a million questions to be asked – questions which people in the United States don't ask about their own communities. They don't know, for example, who owns the newspaper or what the circulation of the newspaper is or who reads it or what people talk about. What are the class percentages, what are the racial divisions, what are the tensions, what are the animosities in this town? This is important information without which you cannot do community development. A Volunteer has got to be trained to get this information. He has got to have courage to knock on doors and listen and eat the food and, when he's through, write it down and pull it together. The key to this stage of community development is social investigation....

Once having made the determination of who his neighbors are and what's going on, the Volunteer has a very vital role to perform, which is to communicate the consensus and acquaint the community without preaching with the ways in which that need can be met. The models he will use in his work to help organize local self-government are not necessarily the formal government organizations we are familiar with – city councils, boards of aldermen or even boards of directors which govern our private business enterprises. Rather, the community organizer may take as examples our informal – but highly organized and self-conscious – groups at the level of the PTA, the service club, the church young people's group, the weekly poker game, the bowling league and the car pool.

As organizations form, this work will lead into the use of the second kind of community development. Volunteer – the community action worker... organizing the building of a school, patching the holes in the road, restringing some wire or tapping into the power line ahead of the meter. This phase of community development requires endless attendance at meetings that don't materialize, going day after day when people say they will attend and do not. It requires not being offended and not becoming impatient: In effect, understanding the culture with which they're dealing. It would be a social insult for a *campesino* to tell a *gringo* that he's not going to come to a meeting in the first place. He says "yes," and so the meeting is scheduled. Twenty-five people said they'd come and two show up, and those two are not among the twenty-five who said they'd come. (Many people come to get out of the cold.) Community action workers must, however, get the twenty-five people together finally, get them to assign themselves tasks while appearing himself in a subordinate and advisory role. This phase is an integral part of community development because it will demonstrate that things can be accomplished by people working together, that the physical tools are available, that at least a structure can be put up or a road can be filled without waiting for the government to do it. And after that, with an appropriate response from the community organizer, the thought will occur to do something else – to form a social club, to get a committee together to call on the Ministry of Education and see where that school teacher is or go to the Ministry of Development and find out why they're not furnishing that bulldozer.

If these are the skills in transmission that a community organizer and often a teacher will need to have, what are the bodies of knowledge that they might be asked to transmit? We expect that these will be public health and personal medical knowledge, languages and literacy, and engineering in the widest sense – that is, the basic technology necessary to improve farming methods and build roads and bridges, chiefly from materials at hand. We will take up the health and engineering matters below; what is necessary to understand is that learning to *teach* these skills will be more important for the Peacemakers to do than simply learning to *use* these skills, and that actually teaching them to others will probably be the most effective way of learning both to teach them and to do them. Learning to teach is of course crucial because once a Peacemaker team leaves some village or barrio, the people left behind must know how to plan and dig an irrigation ditch or a public toilet themselves; and teaching others is generally agreed to be one of the most effective ways of mastering a body of information for one's self.

For all these reasons, it is urgent that the students of the Academy spend a considerable amount of time in "practice" teaching – that is, real teaching of people who are in approximately the same situations as the people they expect to work with as Peacemakers. (This should be kept in mind in choosing a site for the Academy.) There will never be any perfect arrangement along these lines, since the cultural systems of various countries, and therefore responses to different ways of imparting information, will be so different. The multi-cultural backgrounds of the Academy student body as a whole should, for this reason, make the technique of one student practice-teaching others more useful than it has been, for example, to the American Peace Corps; and the multicultural backgrounds of many of the students as individuals should make each of them more flexible as teachers than most volunteers coming from a single-country background. This flexibility should be enhanced by working with textbooks frequently used in and tape recordings made from classes held in some of the major cultures in which the Peacemakers will later be working, and the teaching-training work should therefore be integrated with learning various languages and mores. But practice teaching should still be done in real villages, with real urban slum-dwellers, and among real illiterates.

Technical Skills

The teaching should probably concentrate on medicine and engineering, because in all the likely situations of Peacemaker involvement – natural disasters, violent crises, and chronically troubled areas of poverty – the danger to human health is likely to be high and the general level of machinery and technology likely to be low. Students at the Peacemakers Academy should probably learn the basics of these skills early in their curriculum; then move out into nearby communities in teams under close supervision to teach these basics and in the process to learn more of their specialties; and return to teach each other what they have learned, thus forcing themselves to learn still more. If some students specialize in health problems, some in agricultural engineering, others in structures like roads and dams, and still others in electrical and electronic engineering, the various specialists can be combined upon graduation from the Academy into a highly effective six- to ten-man team. (If married couples are enlisted, the husbands and wives should always specialize in different areas.)

The thirteen-man teams of American Seabees are the nearest equivalent to what we are proposing. They include a graduate engineer, several general equipment operators and mechanics, two builders, an electrician, a steel-worker, a water-systems utilityman, an engineering aid trained in surveying and soil analysis, and a hospital corpsman. Each is trained in construction trades other than his own speciality and in the use of weaponry intended for emergency use in self-defense. In recent years in developing countries they have built small earth dams, roads, piers, ditches, wells, hospitals, schools, bridges, marketplaces, and electrical distribution systems, have run medical and sanitation programs, shown movies and conducted classes in English, *and have worked alongside nationals of the host countries to teach them how to undertake all these kinds of projects*. The one skill not well developed among Seabees that might be required of Peacemakers may be agricultural-improvement work: essentially the county agent's job of knowing and teaching soils and fertilizers and basic agricultural engineering.

In order to train men in the necessary skills, the crucial tangible need is the kind of equipment that will be available in the field. (Each Seabee team has four trucks and two trailers of varying sizes, a water trailer, a concrete mixer, a road grader, a front end loader with back hoe, a tractor, an arc welder, an array of hand tools, and basic medical supplies.) Men who have been selected for aptitude in mechanical improvisation can be turned loose on such equipment under moderate supervision, with real tasks to do, for their training. With such an arrangement, indeed, the students could probably build most of the Academy – reducing costs and making their own education a good deal more real and relevant at the same time.

The training of public-health and medical aids among the Peacemakers should not be seen in terms of the training of American M.D.'s, let alone advanced medical specialists. The Russian *feldsher* is much nearer the intention. For students having eight years of school, the *feldsher* training takes almost four years, and the *feldshers* then are qualified to run a public health program (inoculations against infectious diseases, inspections of possible foci of infection, etc.), teach the public good health practices, give first aid, assist in childbirth, diagnose and treat many minor or fairly routine diseases, and even perform some kinds of surgery. Young people who had already in their own countries received part or all of the training to be *feldshers* (or the auxiliary health personnel who are their equivalents in countries other than the Soviet Union) might be available as students for the Peacemakers Academy, and if one *feldsher* were included in each Peacemaker team, the other members could easily be trained to perform emergency medical services under his direction, when in time of disaster or epidemic or war such services were urgently needed. As a World Health Organization conference at Khartoum on the training of health auxiliary personnel concluded (1961):

> There would seem to be little doubt, that, even in the case of medical assistants, what is called "on the job" training of auxiliaries provides the most important equipment for their future work, and the opinion has been put forward that the time given to the repetition of essential operations until they are assimilated almost as habits by the trainee auxiliary, is time usefully employed. It is preferable for an auxiliary to be thoroughly competent in a few essential manoeuvres than to have a superficial acquaintance and an uncertainty with a greater number....
>
> As to the location of an auxiliary training school, there are several points to be considered, e.g. the medical assistant must have access to hospital training, but it is debatable whether this should be in a large hospital with modern accessories of ward equipment and scientific apparatus, or whether it should be somewhat more in line with the environment of rural areas in which he may have to work and where initiative and improvisation with no one at hand to guide him are the rule... [We would urge the latter. – AIW.]
>
> In methods of teaching "learning by doing" using discussion rather than the didactic system... will doubtless be favoured. Some mass lectures are inevitable but perhaps it will be agreed that these should be kept to a minimum, not an easy recommendation to implement...
>
> A point concerning the living conditions of auxiliaries under training is submitted. The residential school is generally favoured as a method of inculcating good habits in the trainee which may be used as examples to the public.

To summarize the necessary curriculum, therefore, we would sketch a pattern something like this:

Time of Study: When begins, when heavy concentration when ends	Subjects: Elective or Required		
Heavy, Months 1–6; Continues to Month 24	Choice by Students: Languages and Cultures Arabic | Spanish | Urdu | Etc.		
Heavy, Months 1–6; Continues to Month 24	All Students: Police Behavior, including weaponry		
Begins Month 1, Heavy Months 7–12, Continues to Month 24	Choice by Students: Practical Specialities Construction (& teaching it)	Agriculture (& teaching it)	Public Health (& teaching it)
Begins Month 7, Heavy Months 13–18, Continues to Month 24	All Students: Community Organizing (fieldwork near Academy)		
Begins Month 13 Heavy Months 19–24	All Students: Conciliation (using simulation games)		

In the last six months at the Academy, teams would be made up that would be expected to stay together for the next two or three years. These teams would have people who had specialized in different languages and had concentrated in different practical specialties. Thus of a team of 10 (each member of which would have at least three languages), all would speak English; six Arabic as well; four or five French, another four or five Spanish, and five or so would have some other language – possibly one not widely spoken. (It would seem important to make sure that a majority of each team had one language other than English in common. Perhaps the whole team could – so that certain teams would be equipped for total effectiveness instantly on landing in a given trouble zone.) And the group would have an electrician, a *feldsher*, a construction worker, a surveyor, etc.

These teams should probably be set up by the faculty of the Academy, but should probably be allowed to choose their own leaders and leadership methods. They would tend to do so anyway, under the conditions of semi-isolation as a small group in a non-crisis peacekeeping project. Indeed, among the sorts of people created by the training program we propose, rigid hierarchies of command are much less likely to be effective than rather egalitarian decision-making from day to day, within the team. Almost certainly, in a group of ten, one or two persons would become the usual leaders, from whom the majority would normally take their cues (or who would normally formulate and channel majority wishes). In a crisis, when Peacemakers were being sent to an area of violence, a superior command would unify the teams; we will discuss below how such a command could be exercised. If such teams were formed during the last six months' stay at the Academy, egregious errors in assignment could be corrected and the groups could begin to work together before being sent off on their own.

The Institution

The size and shape of the Academy must be seen as a matter of stages. Undoubtedly the world could use 10,000 or 20,000 Peacemakers at any moment, but both the financial resources necessary to train that many men in the next decade and the political support or acceptance necessary to allow the creation of such a sizable transnational force (which would be a major new element in the calculations of international political leaders) are unobtainable.

We must therefore see the Academy as beginning fairly small: with a first-year student body of 275, a second-year size of 525 (assuming about 25 drop-outs during the first year of each entering class). Perhaps the Academy should hold steady at that point for about five years as it begins to prove its worth, reshape its curriculum in accordance with experience, win new support, calm fears, etc. Such an Academy would make available each year after the first a graduating class of about 250, or at least twenty-five teams of Peacemakers. After five years of operation, almost 1,000 men (assuming some 250 would have quit) would be available around the world for Peacemaking duty in emergencies.

It may be useful to look more closely at the several stages of Academy-building, and to that end we shall examine first what the Academy might look like and cost during its first five years in actual operation; and then at the previous stage of planning and creating it.

The Academy in Operation

Each member of the Academy faculty should be highly skilled in several different directions. Most should be multilingual and be trained in social science, have a number of practical technical skills, and be widely experienced. Such men would normally command high prices on the world academic or governmental market. In order to prevent faculty salaries from becoming so expensive as to make the entire Academy impracticable, it may be necessary to think in terms of three- or four-year tours of duty, taken by men out of commitment and out of desire to absorb a new experience, in which their salaries would be reasonable, but lower than they could get on an open market. The Peace Corps salary arrangement along with Peace Corps motivations, would probably work: that is, living facilities would be provided free by the Academy, and most salaries would be paid in a lump sum at the end of a tour of duty. By this arrangement the normal upward social pressure from colleagues toward a higher standard of expenditure would be avoided for the length of the man's tenure. On these conditions a salary of about $9,000 a year might well be acceptable. The faculty should, of course, be drawn from many countries and ideologies; and although a higher proportion of the multi-educated men wanted may be found in highly developed countries with their larger academic, professional, and volunteer institutions, every effort should be made to select faculty from under-developed countries and from countries neutral in major world conflicts.

If we postulate an institution of about 525 students at any given moment, with a ratio of one teacher to every thirteen students, we can begin to assess costs. Forty instructors at an average salary of $9,000 a year would cost $360,000; living expenses for 600 faculty, students, and staff would run, at $15 a week (Spartan living by American standards, but a reasonable level in an under-developed country) $468,000; and equipment and administration would run about $200,000. Total, $1,028,000.* Capital costs cannot easily be assessed; for example, a contribution of land with Spartan housing for about 600 people, plus one building usable for a language laboratory and one classroom building, might be practically enough to begin with, if the students were to build all additional facilities; and the cost of such a contribution would depend very heavily on where in the world it was to be.

Finance is usually closely connected with governance of any institution. Since it seems likely that the private groups able to contribute substantial sums will be chiefly those in the developed world, it may be wise to specify that financial contributions from certain kinds of governments will be accepted and indeed soliticed, to counter-balance contributions from private associations in the developed world. Such contributions ought certainly to come only from those governments not great powers; probably only from those not in the developed world; and perhaps only from those that are neutral in the great world conflicts. Every effort should be made to get commitments for contributions to extend over a three or five-year period, so that direct dependence on the contributors will be lessened.

It should be assumed that the expenses of Peacemaker units made up of Academy alumni would be borne by their host countries, by the inter-

* This figure squares rather well with the estimate of £900 (or about $2500) cost per university student in Tanzania, which for 525 students would come to $1,312,500. J. B. KNIGHT, The Costing and Financing of Educational Development in *Tanzania*, (Unesco: 1966).

national community, or by other means not related to the Academy itself; and in regard to the graduate Peacemakers, the Academy should attempt only to insure that invitations involve *bona fide* peacekeeping operations, not attempts to smash a revolution. To this end, in the absence of a UN invitation the Academy Board might approve a project by a two-thirds vote.

The Planning Stage

The political coloration of the Academy – and its effort at "non-coloration" in regard to all political questions except the desirability for avoiding outright violence and of achieving change without violence – will be heavily determined by the process with which planning it is undertaken and a governing board is chosen. In a sense, it is already regrettable that the initial effort comes chiefly from citizens of North America, and from one of the great powers at that: indeed, that this paper is being written by an American; but this handicap can be surmounted if the Americans involved understand that it must be surmounted *at once*. Citizens of smaller and more neutral states like Algeria, Sweden, Finland, and Cambodia should become central to the planning effort as soon as humanly possible. In addition, members of the United Nations secretariat and a wide spectrum of UN delegations should be involved because of their obvious interest in questions of peacekeeping and the obvious hope that graduates of the Academy will be acceptable as emergency UN Peacemakers. Since the present government of China is not represented in the UN, it is important that efforts should be made through countries and private groups friendly to it to involve the Chinese in planning the Academy.

One possible early step in both planning and creating the Academy might be the holding of a summer planning and training session that would bring together from around the world a number of the people who should be engaged in the Academy itself. If 15 of the sorts of men who should be on the Academy's faculty (a Brazilian engineer, a Canadian UN-force officer, a Tanzanian public-health physician, an Egyptian language teacher, a Burmese Red Cross worker) were brought together with about 15 of the sorts of people who should be its students, the group could both actually begin to do the kind of learning and teaching suitable for the Academy, and propose more detailed answers to a number of questions about its site, size, and form. Many of these people might go right on to become members of the Board, the faculty, and the student body of the Academy. The costs of the summer session would of course be much lower than those of the Academy in actual operation, and potential donors might well fund the summer session first and watch its proceedings to see whether the Academy itself would be likely to succeed and whether, therefore, a larger investment seemed worthwhile.

When a broadly-based planning committee has explored the idea with various interest groups around the world sufficiently to see that enough money and political approval will be forthcoming, a formal governing board for the Academy should be created. The board should naturally include experts in problems of education, peacekeeping, and economic development who are, if possible, representative of all major political interests in the world. It might well be weighted toward the "neutrals," small powers, and international bodies like the UN or its specialized agencies. Provision might be made that graduates of the Academy should, after several years in the field, share in choosing the trustees. Only such a board might be trusted in most of the world to double as not only trustees for the Academy but also as a board of review for bids to use alumni of the Academy in particular projects.

One question that will come before the Board very quickly is the choice of administrators who would actually get the Academy going and who would almost certainly interview and recommend the first faculty. It might be wise to consider pairing two administrators who would join in this task, each from a different kind of "neutral" country and each with some different kind of relevant expertise: perhaps, for example, an expert in peacekeeping from Scandinavia and an expert in grass-roots economic development from a revolutionary African state. The two men might have to agree on all faculty nominees, thus preventing any unintended skewing of the faculty to one or another political view or expertise.

The Site

Another question sure to be among the earliest to be placed before any planning committee or Board will be that of a site for the Academy. It does not follow that a decision need be made in haste; and indeed there are so many factors to be weighted that unless a remarkable site is made available quickly, the decision might well be delayed until other arrangements are complete. The factors include those of symbolic importance of the site (in line with the necessity of building a special *esprit de corps* among the Peacemakers and a special mystique around them); the political weight of various sites; the educational value of locating in an under-developed country and perhaps in one with a chronic internal conflict; the financial attractiveness of possibly more interest from prospective contributors in the developed countries if the Academy were located where they could frequently see it and hear of it; and perhaps others.

On symbolic grounds, for example, Hiroshima might be an outstanding choice for the Academy; on educational grounds, Cyprus; on political grounds, Algeria or Tanzania (two of the few countries in the world that have diplomatic relations with the United States, the Soviet Union, the Western European countries, and China – all four poles of major power in the present world); on some financial grounds, Canada or Scandinavia. All these possibilities should be explored and the various factors given due weight before a final decision is made.

The possibility should also be explored of making the Academy mobile –

perhaps placed aboard one or a few ships that could travel from place to place depending on educational and political needs. A mobile Academy would, for instance, not run the risk of being paralyzed by political disturbances in one country where it happened to be; and its students could get a much deeper and more immediate sense of cultural diversities. The cost of a mobile Academy might, on the other hand, be considerably higher; and it might be hard to train students in real-life situations of conflict or poverty if they were constantly on the move.

If the Academy found new support after about five years in operation, and were therefore able to bring more students and faculty, careful consideration should be given to starting new centers at other places, rather than expanding the original campus. We say this partly for academic reasons. For example, the training in community organization would best be done where the Academy can relate to, but not dominate or wall itself off from, a surrounding community where practice in community organization is possible; and the training in many practical specialties would best be done by building most of the necessary facilities of the Academy itself, in fairly primitive conditions that would not long be preserved if thousands of students had been building a campus for many years instead of starting over in some new locale. In addition, political wisdom would suggest scattering the bases and multiplying the attachments of a transnational organization as soon as that became possible, instead of involving it heavily with a single national government.

The Alumni

At several points above, we have suggested that the Academy will continue to have intimate institutional contacts with its alumni, the graduate Peacemakers. We believe that in many circumstances, the Academy's Board should be responsible for approving or disapproving missions of the Peacemakers (at least where they are invited by some single government, or for that matter some non-governmental organization, rather than by the UN). We believe the Peacemakers might, after several years, help to choose some members of the Academy Board and some of them might, after a number of years in the field, be excellent instructors for the Academy faculty.

We do not, however, believe that the Academy can pay the expenses of its graduates' peacekeeping, peacecreating, or disaster-relief operations. Normally we would expect these expenses to be paid by the UN, the host country (or some other extending it this form of "foreign aid"), or the inviting organization. This raises one problem: can employment be guaranteed the Academy's alumni in advance, if employment is dependent on the decisions of others than the Academy itself? And if not, will this make more difficult the recruitment of students for the Academy?

Efforts should be made when plans for the Academy are definitely set but before it opens its student rolls to applicants, to get tentative agreements from various countries to invite one or more teams of Peacemakers to carry on development projects or conflict-coping tasks after the first class graduates. It may not be possible to get all ten or so teams in the first class accounted for in advance; but if several are, the attraction to students should be strong enough to make a large number of worthy people willing to apply to enter the Academy. Moreover, it seems likely that even if worst came to worst and not all teams could be employed as teams when they left the Academy, many governments and private groups would be delighted to employ people who had been trained to be the multi-capable people that the Academy ought to be training. These alumni would, indeed, constitute a kind of "world service corps" – teachers, engineers, public-health nurses, translators – that would be useful as international civil servants for the UN and its specialized agencies even if they never dealt with a violent crisis. They might be put on "stand-by" duty in national projects; if they stayed in teams, these stand-bys could quickly be transferred to international duty.

Once placed in development projects, local conflict areas, and other such work, the Peacemakers would be available for emergency service for the UN. If they were called to duty by UN, a command structure more formal than that created by each team for itself would be necessary. Presumably over-all military or political direction would be provided by the UN itself through the Secretariat, as is usual in UN peacekeeping operations. In some circumstances, the Peacemakers might be a sufficient force and might serve alone. (In Yemen, for example, in 1963 the UN sent about 200 observers; in West Irian, in 1962, about 1500; in Lebanon, in 1958, 100; in Kashmir, in 1948, about 100.) In many other circumstances, much larger numbers of men might be needed than would be available during the first five years of the Academy; and in such circumstances, the Peacemakers might well expect to serve alongside or perhaps to help in commanding earmarked military forces or emergency units supplied the UN by member countries. We should emphasize that we do not expect the Peacemakers to be fully interchangeable with conventional UN military forces made up of seconded national units in the near or even middle future; we do expect there will be many situations they are better equipped to handle, as well as some they ought not to try to handle at all.

Conclusion

No report of the problems to be faced or the opportunities to be sought in founding such an institution as the one proposed here can substitute for the ingenuity and political wisdom that will be required of any planning committee that tries to create the Academy. There are some subjects on which our preliminary explorations already indicate there will be considerable difference of opinion, and on which our recommendations may turn out to be wrong. For example, it may be that the Academy would benefit more from close proximity to an existing Univeristy on which it can draw for experts, books, etc., than it would from the educational experience involved in having students build the Academy itself almost from scratch. Or again, it may be that traditional military hierarchies would work better in the Peacemaker teams than allowing them to choose their own leader. We do not believe such difference of opinion on particulars invalidates the idea of the Academy in general. Indeed, we should say once more as we have so many times above that experience not only may, but is *certain* to prove parts of this proposal incorrect, and that the success of a venture such as this depends upon willingness to revise the image of the future with which the enterprise begins.

We have not tried to propose an institution that could deal with every international crisis that we expect to occur in the next few decades. We have proposed a way of dealing with *some* such crises, and hopefully of preventing some from erupting. We believe that the existence of a transnational Academy and a corps of Peacemakers of the kind we propose might initiate a kind of social fallout in other areas of international tension or opportunity so that, for example, transnational corps of space explorers, conservation workers, and other sorts of problem-solvers might come to seem more feasible once the Peacemakers Academy was in operation.

But the need for effective peacekeeping is so urgent and the central nature of the issue so apparent that we would urge great effort to be put into beginning the process we have sketched. We can well imagine that if such an

Academy and such Peacemakers had been in existence a decade ago, the conflicts that have festered on the Arab-Israeli borders these last ten years might have been partly reduced; that the particular confrontation over the Gulf of Aqaba that touched off the 1967 war might therefore never have occurred, since it originated partly in response to the border skirmishing in and near Syria; and that even if it had, a transnational force of Peacemakers that the UN would have been freer to use might have been able to deal both effectively and fairly with the Aqaba confrontation. Or to take two other kinds of case: a transnational force of Peacemakers might have been able greatly to increase the political difficulties facing the United States in undertaking its armed intervention in the Dominican Republic – and so to have prevented that intervention; we can imagine that the Peacemakers might have been able to prevent the blood bath of Ibos that began corrosion and disintegration of Nigeria's social fabric.

All these possibilities depend on *time:* time to deal with the social issues before they erupt into war. How likely, then, that ten years hence we will wish the Academy had been founded in 1967! And how likely that if we found it soon, we can the sooner see emerge the conditions on which our children can begin to build a livable world order!

GPSR Compliance

The European Union's (EU) General Product Safety Regulation (GPSR) is a set of rules that requires consumer products to be safe and our obligations to ensure this.

If you have any concerns about our products, you can contact us on ProductSafety@springernature.com

In case Publisher is established outside the EU, the EU authorized representative is:

Springer Nature Customer Service Center GmbH
Europaplatz 3
69115 Heidelberg, Germany

Batch number: 10843651

Printed by Printforce, the Netherlands